WOULD YOU RATHER? VIKINGS

First published in Great Britain 2023 by Red Shed, part of Farshore

An imprint of HarperCollins*Publishers*
1 London Bridge Street, London SE1 9GF
www.farshore.co.uk

HarperCollins*Publishers*
Macken House, 39/40 Mayor Street Upper,
Dublin 1, D01 C9W8

Written by Clive Gifford
Illustrated by Tim Wesson

Copyright © HarperCollins*Publishers* Limited 2023

ISBN 978 0 00 852179 0

Printed and bound in the UK using 100% Renewable Electricity at CPI Group (UK) Ltd.

001

A CIP catalogue record for this title is available from the British Library.

MIX
Paper | Supporting
responsible forestry
FSC™ C007454

This book is produced from independently certified FSC™ paper
to ensure responsible forest management.

For more information visit: www.harpercollins.co.uk/green

CLIVE GIFFORD • TIM WESSON

WOULD YOU RATHER? VIKINGS

RED SHED

Contents

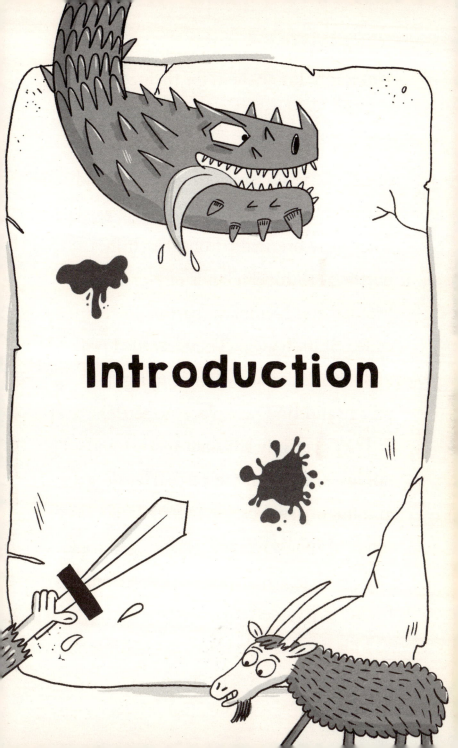

Introduction

You might know them for their cool helmets and bushy beards – but the Vikings were more than that! They were one of the most ferocious, fearsome and formidable groups of people in the world. They were originally from the chilly northern-European lands of Norway, Sweden and Denmark (part of an area called Scandinavia). They travelled near and far on spectacular ships to fight, pillage and find new places to settle.

They certainly left their mark – and not just scars from their lethal battle-axes and mighty swords. They found new river routes through Europe, encouraged trade and developed incredible crafts – from beautiful jewellery to magnificent ships.

This book is filled with fascinating

SCANDINAVIA & NORTHERN EUROPE

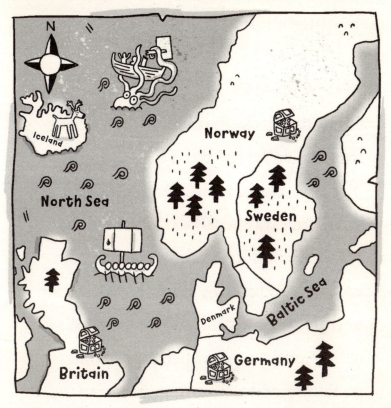

facts, fun challenges and mind-boggling 'would you rather' questions, that will teleport you back into the incredible Viking world. Get ready to discover what life was really like there!

Are you ready?

How it all started

Up to the fifth century CE, the ancient Romans ruled the roost in Europe, North Africa and the Middle East. But, their time was nearly up – trouble within the Roman Empire and pressure from invaders caused this HUGE civilization to collapse. This meant that land was up for grabs – many different peoples started moving, invading, battling and settling all across the area the Romans had ruled over. Can you guess what one of these groups was? Yep, the Vikings! They started out in Scandinavia, but soon began invading other areas, too.

Compared to the regimented Romans with their single emperor, the Vikings weren't all that settled and organised. Rather than one big empire, there were many smaller groups of Vikings, each with their own leader.

Vikings were raiders and traders – no way were they settling for a quiet life in Scandinavia. Many Viking groups grabbed their swords or precious goods and sailed all over Europe, even as far afield as Asia and North Africa. These groups mixed in different ways with the settlers they met – making for some very different Viking towns across the world.

So, pick up your oars, grab your axe, and let's sail off into the unknown . . .

WOULD YOU RATHER

sail the seas as a Viking raider

OR a Viking trader?

SCANDINAVIA MIGHT HAVE BEEN THE VIKINGS' HOME, BUT THE SEA CAME A CLOSE SECOND! THEY SPENT HUGE AMOUNTS OF TIME BOBBING AROUND ON THE WAVES – EVEN THE WORD 'VIKING' ITSELF MEANS 'PIRATE'! BUT, THE REASONS THAT VIKINGS JUMPED ON THEIR LONGSHIPS TO SAIL INTO THE SUNSET COULD BE VERY DIFFERENT ...

Raider

Decided to go for the ferocious raiding option? Hope you don't need much alone time – you'd be crammed into a narrow, sleek wooden Viking longship around 15–20m long with up to 30–40 other raiders who definitely didn't use deodorant. Let's take a look at your boat!

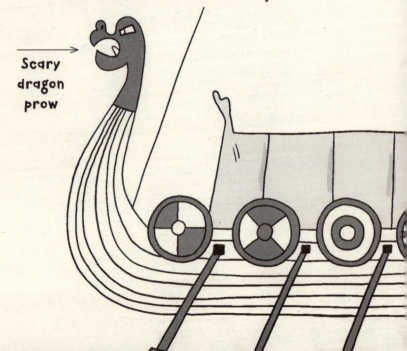

Scary dragon prow

Wind flag

Buckets for bailing out water in rough seas

Sail (made of linen cloth)

Sacks of food and (hopefully) more sacks of treasure on the return journey

Wooden mast (could be lowered when super-stormy)

Shields

Oars

15

Once your ship was built, stocked and good to go, you'd be ready to raid, huzzah! Viking ships were fast and easy to manoeuvre, and could land directly onto beaches rather than needing a harbour – useful for keeping that all-important element of surprise. Vikings could land anywhere, and sneak up on towns or villages on foot. Boo!

The raid leader may have sent frenzied berserkers (see page 144) ahead to confuse and panic the enemy whilst the rest of the group got into formation. Raiders would cram together to form a tight rectangle, with their shields overlapping to protect the fighters at the front and shields behind raised like a roof to stop arrows. They would fight from behind these protective shield walls, skewering the enemy with pointy spears or hacking off the odd arm, leg or head.

The ultimate goal? Treasure! The best targets were churches, halls and finer buildings, as they were likely to hold lovely shiny gold and silver. If you survived, you could be rich, rich, rich!

church
PET
SHOP

Trader

Prefer to get your goods by dealing rather than stealing? Many Vikings didn't fancy getting a limb chopped off on a raid, so chose a more peaceful option. They traded goods from their travels, for other items, amounts of silver or gold (called bullion), or coins.

Vikings had lots of goods to trade that others around the world needed – but traders drive a hard bargain. You'd

need a haul of top-quality goods on your ship to trade for local items . . .

PACKING LIST

- FURS (MAYBE FOX OR BEAR, GOOD FOR KEEPING WARM)

- IRON TOOLS

- WHALEBONE (GOOD FOR CARVING ORNAMENTS)

- WEAPONS (LIKE SHARP SWORDS - SEE PAGE 56)

- JEWELLERY

Once they had packed their chests, it was time to plan a route . . .

As the Vikings flourished, they explored more and more of Europe and beyond. Their travels took them across the North Sea to what is now northern France, Germany, England and Ireland. Some headed across the Baltic Sea to Russia and sailed along rivers deep into eastern Europe. With all this moving around, trade was booming!

By the late ninth century CE, Viking traders were EVERYWHERE. Well, almost. They had reached Spain, the Mediterranean Sea and even North Africa and Asia.

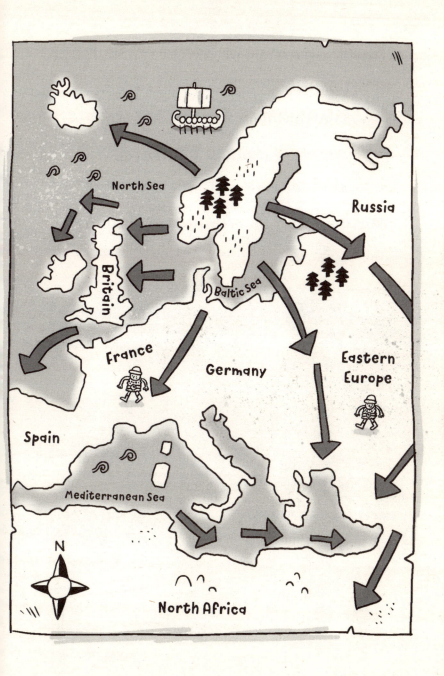

North Sea

Russia

Britain

Baltic Sea

France

Germany

Eastern Europe

Spain

Mediterranean Sea

N

North Africa

21

Travelling to new places gave them heaps of new goods to sell – result! Spices from North Africa and the Middle East, for example, became a Viking trader's dream. They weighed little, but were worth a lovely, heavy amount of money.

This might sound like the perfect money-making plan – but being a trader wasn't all plain sailing. You'd need to look out as you might be robbed at sea by pirates, or cheated on land by dodgy-dealing traders. Many Viking traders carried their own set of weights and folding scales, so they could check they weren't being conned.

Can you *sea* yourself as a sailor? Or would you prefer to *wave* boats goodbye altogether?

VIKING EXTRAS
Eat like a Viking

As a hard-working Viking, you'd be in need of some hearty meals to keep you going! The Vikings ate two meals a day, in the morning and evening (no lunch for them). The *dagverðr* was a late breakfast eaten after they had been up and working for several hours. That's 7 or 8am by the way – the Vikings rose early! It would probably be porridge, or bread with leftovers from the night before.

The *náttverðr*, or night meal, was usually a stew made in a cauldron heated by fire. This was eaten straight after finishing work in the evening by which time Vikings were STARVING.

Sometimes, it may have paid not to know what you were eating . . . here are a few unusual Viking delicacies!

Whale of a time

Finding a whale was quite an event for Vikings. They didn't have whaling ships, so it's more likely they attacked whales that had been beached on shorelines or

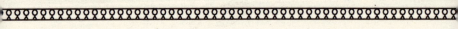

had swum up river inlets by mistake. Whales would be set upon by a whole village who would often fight over who had the rights to the whale's meat and fatty blubber (which could be used to make oil that was burned in lamps). If you and your family were lucky, you'd get a big chunk of whale to do with as you pleased!

Birds for breakfast

The Vikings were pretty resourceful when it came to finding wildlife to eat. Reindeer, seals, walruses, elk and boar all had to look out, as the Vikings saw them as extremely tasty meals.

Birds weren't safe either. Scandinavia's rocky coastal areas are home to thousands of puffins – small sea birds with colourful beaks. Some of them,

though, ended up frying rather than flying, and became a treat for any brave Vikings hardy enough to clamber over razor-sharp rocks to catch them. The puffin-pursuers would need a head for heights . . . some stood on the very edge of a cliff and used a long-handled net called a *hafur* to catch the birds. If they were successful, they could bag dozens of puffins a day. One slip though would mean a swift and spiky tumble . . .

Some Vikings preferred to eat the birds' eggs rather than the puffins themselves – definitely easier to catch!

Recipe for Rotting Shark

Some Vikings preferred a toothier snack. Here is a Viking method for preparing jaw-some rotting shark!

CLEAN AND GUT A SHARK, THEN PLACE IT IN A SHALLOW HOLE OF SAND AND GRAVEL.

BURY IT UNDER A PILE OF HEAVY ROCKS AND STONES. (SOME ACCOUNTS SAY THAT ALL THE PEOPLE IN A VIKING SETTLEMENT WEED ON THE SHARK BEFORE IT WAS BURIED. CHARMING!)

LEAVE YOUR SHARK THERE FOR BETWEEN 6–12 WEEKS. REMEMBER WHERE YOU BURIED IT! WHEN THE STINKY SHARK IS GOOD AND READY, DIG IT UP, SLICE IT INTO STRIPS AND HANG IT TO DRY FOR A FEW MONTHS.

THEN, AND ONLY THEN, COULD THE PUNGENT MEAT BE EATEN. MMMMMM. THIS DISH IS STILL SOMETIMES PREPARED IN ICELAND TODAY, WHERE IT IS CALLED HÁKARL.

Bonus fact:

Some shark meat is poisonous! Letting it rot and ferment for months actually made it safer to eat.

WOULD YOU RATHER

play Viking tug of war

OR throw bones at your dinner guests?

WHEN THEY WEREN'T FIGHTING OR FEASTING, VIKINGS WOULD COME UP WITH ALL KINDS OF GAMES TO ENTERTAIN THEMSELVES, BOTH OUTSIDE AND IN THEIR HOMES. SOME COULD GET PRETTY ROUGH AND ROWDY!

Tug of war

Have you got a good sense of balance and some massive muscles to flex? Toga Honk might be just your thing. This was the Viking version of tug of war – two opponents would grip a loop at either end of a length of rope, and try to pull their opponent past a line drawn in the ground between them.

A more deadly version was sometimes used to settle disputes between tribes. Rather than going for an all-out war, both sides would pick just one man. They would each be tied to one end of a rope and stand apart with their backs facing each other. In front of each Viking, just out of reach, was a sword planted into the ground. A life-or-death tug of war then took place, with each Viking trying to reach their sword first, so they could turn and swiftly stab their opponent. Eek!

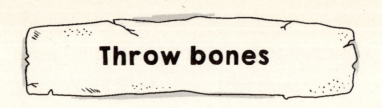

Throw bones

So you've gone for target practice?
Think you could chuck a bone across
a busy dining hall with grace and ease?
Hnútukast is the game for you!

Hnútukast was played after a feast.
The concept was simple – chucking
bones at other Vikings. This might

sound harmless, but the aim of the game was to hurt a fellow diner. Vikings could lose an eye – or even their life – from a big, heavy bone to the bonce. Ouch!

Are you ready for a throwing bone-anza? It might even be good practice for feasts in Valhalla. **Turn to page 110 for more . . .**

Viking leaders hall of fame

There were many kingdoms in the Viking world, led by many powerful kings! They would be in charge of keeping their thralls in order (see page 62), organising raids and generally keeping up a brave, bold and beefy image. The Vikings also had it covered when it came to exciting names . . . read on to discover some of the most legendary Viking leaders!

Eric Bloodaxe

Eric Bloodaxe was the son of King
Harald Finehair (he obviously had found
a good hairdresser), who ruled over
a large part of what is now Norway. It is
said that Harald had as many as 20 sons,
and as he got older, there was quite a lot
of jostling for who would take his place.

Eric had a clear idea of who it should
be: HIM! So, he practised his evil laugh
and began bumping off his brothers and
half-brothers, one by one, to increase his

chances of becoming King. By 931CE, nearly all of them were dead, and Eric took over as ruler – but he didn't last long. He was such a severe king that within a couple of years, his subjects had put their feet down. They rebelled and put one of Eric's surviving brothers, Haakon the Good, on the throne. He had a much more promising name!

Erik the Red

What colour hair do you think this Erik had? You guessed it! Well, probably – it's hard to be absolutely certain, as we don't have any of his actual hair to look at . . .

Erik's full name was Erik Thorvaldsson. He moved to Iceland as a ten year old with his father, Thorvald (who was fleeing for bumping off someone in Norway). Fiery tempers seemed to run in the family as Erik later got in trouble for killing a Viking called Eyjolf the Foul. Erik the Red? More like Erik the Seeing-Red!

Erik sailed a ship far west of Iceland to reach Greenland around 982CE. He and his crew spent two years exploring parts

of this giant, chilly island. On returning home to Iceland, Erik did a great job of bigging up Greenland – even coming up with the name to make it sound like a lovely, grassy, definitely not freezing place to live. It wasn't long before a fleet of Viking ships set off to settle there. Despite hardships, as many as 6,000 Vikings lived in Greenland a generation later – including Erik's son, Leif. Turn the page to hear more about him . . .

Leif Erikson

In the late tenth century CE, Leif Erikson happily sailed away from Greenland to Norway to serve the Viking king there, Olaf Tryggvason. But, on his way back a few years later, he got terribly, terribly lost . . .

Storms and strong winds blew Leif's ship seriously off-course. So off-course, that he ended up becoming the first European to visit mainland North America. Leif named it Vinland, as he had found grapes growing there ('vin' meaning 'wine', made from grapes).

Leif was a bit of a trendsetter, and other Vikings are believed to have made similar trips shortly afterwards, including two of Leif's brothers and a small group originally from Iceland.

Some people scoffed at the idea that Vikings reached North America almost 500 years before the Italian explorer, Christopher Columbus. But in the 1960s, archaeologists discovered ruins of a settlement in Newfoundland, Canada that is dated as 1,000 years old and appears to be made by Vikings. Amazeballs!

Cnut the Great

Most kings are perfectly happy ruling over one country. King Cnut, however, was NOT, and had his sights set on *much* bigger things, thank you very much. During his life, he was king of England, Denmark, Norway and part of Sweden. A big Viking job!

Unlike some other Viking kings, Cnut was a Christian, meaning he worshipped one god rather than lots of Viking pagan gods (see page 120 for more on them). He even went on a trip to visit the Pope in Rome in 1027!

King Cnut is probably best known for the tale of Cnut and the Waves (Disclaimer: it is not completely clear if this is a true story). Cnut is said to have taken his throne down to the seashore and ordered the incoming tide to stop before it reached him. Unsurprisingly, it didn't. Even though Cnut ended up with some very soggy toes, it did help him get his Christian view across to all the baffled onlookers that God's power is greater than a king's. Result!

Told you so...

Thyra Dannebod

As you may have noticed, most of the big shots in the Viking world were men – basically all of them, in fact. But, there were a few powerful women around, including Thyra, queen of Denmark during the tenth century CE.

Most Viking women led a fairly quiet life, running their homes, caring for children, maybe managing the family farm or business if their husband was away on a raid (see page 94). According to some stories, however, Thyra had military matters on her mind. Wanting to protect Denmark from invasion from the south, she is said to have ordered work to be done on a huge barricade called the Danevirke, between Denmark and what is now northern Germany. Parts can still be seen today.

Thyra was also known (as is often the case) for her male relatives – and their not very complimentary names. Thyra was married to Gorm the Old (bet he was thrilled about that nickname). Their son was Harald Bluetooth. Historians think he might have been called this because he had a blue, rotting tooth. Yuck!

So, who gets YOUR crown for most epic Viking leader?

WOULD YOU RATHER

lose your sword on a raid

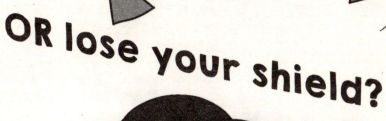

OR lose your shield?

ONCE THEY HAD CROSSED THE SEAS ON THEIR LONGSHIPS, VIKING RAIDERS WOULD HEAD ASHORE, WAVING THEIR WEAPONS READY TO FIGHT OFF ANY PESKY REBELS THEY MIGHT COME ACROSS. TURN OVER TO HAVE A LOOK AT A TYPICAL RAIDER'S OUTFIT BEFORE YOU MAKE YOUR CHOICE...

Viking raider outfit

OK, let's be honest. In the heat of battle, you wouldn't want to lose either your main weapon or your way of defending yourself. But before you decide, let's take a closer look at a Viking raider's kit . . .

Battle axe
(wickedly sharp)

Metal helmet (they did NOT have horns)

Long cloak (for even longer winter months)

Double-edged sword and scabbard (for storing sword when not in use)

Chain mail armour (stab resistant)

Shield

Now, on to your choice!

Lose the sword

Think you'd rather lose the sword and keep your shield? This could be a wise decision – normal Viking armour was made of padded leather which was pretty puny against sharp swords. If you were wealthy, you might upgrade to a chain mail tunic made of metal rings all linked together. But, leather or metal, the Viking's body armour didn't protect them that much – so they really relied on their shields for protection.

This was held in the hand and used to fend off blows as well as arrows whizzing through the air. The shield was circular, made of planks of thin wood and with an

iron mound in the middle called a boss –
a handy bonus weapon for bashing heads!

A Viking's shield was a truly
multi-purpose bit of kit. It could also
be used for bulldozing enemy soldiers
out of the way or pushing them over
walls. Shields could also turn into useful
stretchers to carry the injured away for
treatment . . . or burial.

Lose the shield

Think attack is the best form of defence? You'd definitely not be alone! There were few things a Viking raider cared for more than his sword – and that sometimes included his wife and children. Awkward. For many Vikings lucky enough to afford one, it was their most precious and expensive possession. Some cost more than a dozen dairy cows – an absolute fortune for most Vikings.

A Viking sword was around one metre long and DEADLY. They were forged by blacksmiths from several rods of iron twisted and beaten together. This made them flexible so they didn't shatter when they struck shields or enemy's skulls. Most were double edged, making them perfect for slashing in battle.

Think the raiding life sounds like a looting hoot? Turn to page 144 to hear about the most ferocious raiders!

VIKING EXTRAS
Viking medicine

You *really* wouldn't want to get ill in Viking times – however old you were. There were no doctors or hospitals and little medical knowledge, so you'd likely have to cross your fingers that your body healed by itself. Good luck!

Here are a few Viking remedies . . .

Prayers or rituals

Vikings believed that their gods had the power to heal them when they were sick. They would pray to gods to encourage them to help while the injured or ill Viking rolled around groaning. Eir, the goddess of healing was a favourite target.

Tasting blood

The Vikings knew that putting broken bones back in their rightful place and strapping them up would help them heal. So far so good. But, they also believed that tasting blood from wounds could reveal how serious the injury was. Yuck! It's still not clear why they thought this.

Medicine

Vikings often made infusions of herbs soaked in mead or wine. Most would have been useless – but the odd potion may have worked. The Vikings used the herb horehound, for example, which can help soothe coughs and sore throats and is used in some throat lozenges today.

Runes

Some Vikings used pieces of stone or bone carved with runes as lucky charms to protect them from illness, or help them heal faster. You could give it a try next time you've got a *rune*-y nose . . .

Bonus fact:

Viking families sometimes took brutal decisions. They prided themselves on physical strength, so a sick, weak child was thought of as a bad thing. Some families chose to throw these children overboard into the sea, or abandon them in the wilderness.

WOULD YOU RATHER

have the responsibilities of a wealthy Jarl

OR the chores of a lowly thrall?

IN VIKING TIMES, THE JARLS WERE THE BIG SHOTS. THEY WERE THE RICHEST, MOST POWERFUL PEOPLE IN A LOCAL AREA. THRALLS, ON THE OTHER HAND, WERE PENNILESS SLAVES. UNLUCKY FOR THEM – OR WAS IT? JARLS MIGHT HAVE HAD A MORE COMFY TIME OF IT, BUT MONEY CAN BRING ITS OWN TROUBLE ...

Jarl

Seems like you think riches, power and status are the way to go – lording it over Viking society, having servants to attend your every need . . . why would you not, right? Well, actually, being a Jarl could have its own stresses . . .

JARL'S TO-DO LIST

TALK TO CARPENTER ABOUT BUILDING NEW LONG-HOUSE (VIKING HOME). Make it EXTRA LONG!!!

BUY SOME MORE EPIC VIKING JEWELLERY.

ORGANISE HUGE FEAST. ← Must remember to get extra whale steaks

INSPECT FARMLAND (LOOKED AFTER BY SLAVES AND FREE MEN).

VISIT SHIPBUILDERS TO SEE HOW FLEET OF TRADING SHIPS IS PROGRESSING.

Answering the door is a nightmare!

As a Jarl, you'd need to stay alert and on the look out for envious, sneaky Vikings trying to steal your wealth – many kept it buried underground to hide it. You might also have to deal with the problems of people who lived on your land – maybe even handing out some money to keep them sweet. On top of that, bad harvests could easily cause you to lose all your wealth, maybe even force you to go back to raiding and invading!

Thrall

If you were a thrall, you'd find yourself plonked right at the bottom of Viking society with zero power or privilege. But, with no land or money, you'd have few responsibilities. Phew!

Though this might sound awesome, don't get too excited. You would likely be given the worst jobs around the house or on the farm. Thralls were slaves, mostly captured by Viking raiders and

bought and sold just like cows, chickens or sheep. If they misbehaved, they could expect a thorough beating – so you'd need to stay on your owner's good side!

You might get lucky though – some thralls had kinder owners who either paid them a small amount or, after years of service, granted them their freedom. Woohoo!

Think being a thrall would be totally *en-thralling*? Of course, if you'd rather take on a different sort of Viking life, you can always check out the jobs board on page 136!

VIKING EXTRAS
Find your Viking name

Now you've learned the names of some of the great Viking rulers, let's find out what YOUR Viking name would be . . .

Day

1 – Harald	17 – Torsten
2 – Freyja	18 – Ulfhild
3 – Leif	19 – Frode
4 – Bodil	20 – Gunhild
5 – Knud	21 – Ulf
6 – Hod	22 – Liv
7 – Sven	23 – Inga
8 – Estrid	24 – Bo
9 – Erik	25 – Saga
10 – Frigga	26 – Sif
11 – Njal	27 – Ivar
12 – Ebbe	28 – Ubbe
13 – Yrsa	29 – Tove
14 – Rune	30 – Arne
15 – Hilda	31 – Ursa
16 – Gudrun	

The name next to the day of your birthday below is your Viking first name. The name next to the month is your surname!*

Month

January
Baggy-trousers

February
Speedy-sword

March
Word-master

April
Smelly-stew

May
Foul-fart

June
Nanny-goat

July
Soupy-beard

August
Shaggy-pants

September
Red-beard

October
Lumpy-porridge

November
Loud-snore

December
Dream-decoder

*These names are just for fun, rather than real Viking names!

WOULD YOU RATHER

suffer a trial by fire

OR a trial by water?

THEY MIGHT HAVE BEEN AN UNRULY BUNCH AWAY FROM HOME, BUT BACK IN SCANDINAVIA, THE VIKINGS HAD STRICT LAWS – AND HARSH PUNISHMENTS! ALL RULES (AND THE FATE OF RULE-BREAKERS) WERE DECIDED BY THE THING – WHAT'S A THING, YOU SAY? TURN THE PAGE TO FIND OUT MORE BEFORE YOU MAKE YOUR CHOICE...

The Thing

As a quick pause before you get to your trial (phew!), let's take a look at Viking law courts . . .

Any crimes, from stealing sheep to calling another Viking a coward in public (rude), might result in a trial at a local assembly called a Thing. Yes, a Thing.

The Thing was a bit like a modern law court – just held on top of a mound, with fewer wigs and very different laws. The Thing would choose the fate

of each accused person – but if they couldn't decide if the suspect was guilty or not, they might call for a trial by ordeal. These trials were developed from

Christian beliefs and practice, and were popular in later Viking communities, many of whom had converted to Christianity. There were several kinds of ordeal . . . turn the page to get started!

Trial by fire

So you think you can handle the heat? Is swimming not your Viking Thing? Let's look at a trial by fire . . .

STEP 1

For men: pick up a red-hot iron bar.

For women: plunge hands into a cauldron of boiling water and pick up hot stones from the bottom. Owww!

STEP 2

After this scalding challenge, both men and women had to walk forward a set number of paces, while the painfully hot object burned their hands. If they dropped it they were said to be guilty!

STEP 3

Even if the suspect managed to complete this walk, their trial *still* wasn't over. Their burnt hands would be bandaged up and then their burn wounds examined a few days later. If they were slowly healing then they were considered innocent. But, if the wounds had got infected (pretty likely considering the lack of clean dressings, hospitals etc), then they were guilty!

Trial by water

Are you more of a cool cucumber than a hot potato? Trial by water was definitely a wetter (if not better) option!

STEP 1

The suspect's hands or feet would be bound together with rope. If they were really unlucky (or they'd gone for a wee on their neighbours' cabbages a few too many times), it might be both their hands and feet.

STEP 2

Their body was then tied to a long rope.

STEP 3

They'd then be tossed into a deep lake, river or sea in front of a crowd of onlookers. If they floated, they were guilty – and in even more trouble . . .

Vikings thought if the person sank, it meant the water had accepted them: God's way of believing them to be innocent. If everyone agreed, the suspect would be pulled out of the water (hopefully *before* they drowned).

Of course, in Viking times, suspects wouldn't actually have had a choice in their trial . . . unlucky for them. It could have been worse though - head to page 130 to hear about trials by combat!

VIKING EXTRAS
Dos and don'ts for Viking women

Like many ancient civilisations, Viking society was dominated by men – mostly big burly ones who were good in a fight. Life as a Viking woman would definitely have had its challenges – but it wasn't all bad. Here are a few things that Viking women could (and couldn't) get up to . . .

Go on raids

Absolutely not. Sailing across the seven seas wielding axes and terrorising people was definitely man territory.

Run a farm?

Go for it! If you were a Viking woman and your husband was away (berserking, pillaging, raiding etc), you would probably take *goat*-al responsibility of the family farm and finances.

Become a ruler of a kingdom?

Sadly, not (though there were a few exceptions – see page 48). Most women couldn't even take part in decision making about their local communities.

Own property

Sure!

Wear men's clothes?

Hmm, I think not . . . Vikings had clear ideas about what men and women should wear. Men wore wool trousers with a tunic over the top. Most Viking women on the other hand wore a dress with a linen petticoat underneath. Some Viking kingdoms even had laws against women wearing men's clothes and cutting their hair short!

Get divorced

Yep – ditch that rubbish husband! Viking women were welcome to divorce. One is said to have got rid of her husband because he leapt around bare-chested all the time. Seems fair.

The divorcing process was simple. The woman would find a couple of witnesses and announce that she was divorced. Easy! However, the process of dividing up property may have been trickier, especially if they were rich.

It's over.

I'll keep the house and the farm, hopefully you can keep your shirt on for five minutes.

WOULD YOU RATHER

write as a Saxon scribe

OR recite as a Viking poet?

ARE YOU A MASTER WORDSMITH? THINK YOUR HANDWRITING IS PRETTY NEAT? IN THE TIMES OF THE VIKINGS AND SAXONS, THERE WERE NO PRINTED BOOKS OR MAGAZINES. IMPORTANT INFORMATION WAS PASSED FROM PERSON TO PERSON THROUGH SPEECH, OR COPIED OUT SLOWLY AND PAINSTAKINGLY BY HAND ... HOPE YOU'VE GOT STRONG QUILL-POWER!

Saxon scribe

So, you think being a scribe sounds pretty ink-redible? To be a Saxon scribe, you were most likely VERY religious and worked in a monastery (a building for monks). This was because most writing work at the time was copying out Christian works like the Bible onto vellum, a material made from calf skin.

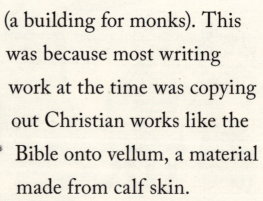

It wouldn't have been the *most* comfortable job. Your workplace would have been a chilly, draughty monastery room, lit mostly by daylight – cross your fingers for sunshine! Your (likely shivering) bottom would have been plonked on a hard, wooden seat all day as you carefully copied out each letter in your very neatest handwriting. A single book might take a year or more to create – so you'd better get it *write*!

Don't despair though, there would be some perks. You'd have a roof over your head, fellow monks to hang out with and lots of peace and quiet. (Just remember to pray no marauding Vikings drop by – see page 100!)

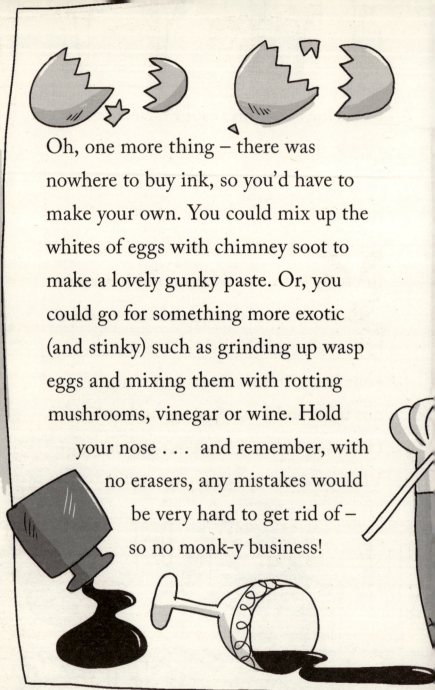

Oh, one more thing – there was nowhere to buy ink, so you'd have to make your own. You could mix up the whites of eggs with chimney soot to make a lovely gunky paste. Or, you could go for something more exotic (and stinky) such as grinding up wasp eggs and mixing them with rotting mushrooms, vinegar or wine. Hold your nose . . . and remember, with no erasers, any mistakes would be very hard to get rid of – so no monk-y business!

Viking poet

Have you got a *rap*-titude for rhyme?
Think you could thrill a thrall and
captivate a king with your awesome
public speaking? Viking poetry might
just be for you!

Compared to the Saxons, the Vikings
weren't big writers – they preferred
sword-slashing and chucking bones at
each other (see page 32). But, they *were*
suckers for a good story – and skalds, or
professional poets, were the people for
the job.

Skalds needed a memory as epic as
a Viking saga – they would have to
recount loooong poems and even longer

stories from memory, without any books or scrolls to help them. And, they'd need to be fun and fascinating enough to avoid sending their audience into a big Scandinavian snooze.

As a skald, you might work for one particular Jarl (see page 62) or king, or be hired by different people. Feasts at a Jarl's hall could be tough gigs. Many guests wouldn't give a puffin's pyjamas about poetry and would be MUCH more interested in gobbling up as much grub as they could manage!

Some Vikings were TERRIBLE poets who were not thanked for going on a stanza bonanza. But there was an explanation for why some poets were bad . . . find out on page 127.

VIKING EXTRAS
Write your own poem

How are your poetry skills? Why not try creating your own Viking verse? Copy out the lines opposite on a spare piece of paper, filling in the gaps with words from the bottom of the page to make four pairs of rhyming lines – or just pick your own words!

Bonus fact:

A handful of Viking poets were also super-tough warriors. The most famous was Egil Skallagrimsson. It was said that he started his career writing and fighting as a warrior-poet by the age of nine – scary!

There once was a Viking called _____

Who let out the smelliest _____

There once was a Viking called _____

Who'd got a ring stuck on her _____

A cheery young Viking called _____

Once whistled a musical _____

There once was a Viking called _____

Who ate fourteen puffins each _____

Bart*   day   Frey

Rune   fart   Inge

finger   tune

*not a Viking name

WOULD YOU RATHER

stay at home as a Viking farmer

OR take to the seas as a Viking raider?

THE VIKINGS STARTED OUT MERRILY TENDING THEIR TURNIPS AS FARMERS IN DENMARK, SWEDEN AND NORWAY. BUT EVENTUALLY, SOME DECIDED TO DITCH THEIR PITCHFORKS. THERE WERE RICHES AND EXCITING NEW HOMES TO BE FOUND, BY SETTING SAIL TO RAID AND BATTLE ABROAD!

Farmer

So you're not so sure about sailing off into the sunset to unknown lands? Not into stealing, hacking off other people's arms and legs or living with 30 smelly men in a cramped longship for weeks at a time? Understandable – there were plenty of reasons not to go raiding.

Many Vikings were peaceful, stay-at-home types. Some worked as traders, craftspeople or blacksmiths, most were farmers on small amounts of land.

This might sound idyllic – quiet, open spaces, peaceful woods, clucking chickens . . . but not so fast. Much of the Vikings' home territory in Scandinavia wasn't the best farmland. Farmers had to learn quickly what crops grew well and stockpile enough grub to survive the harsh winters. Remember, there were no potatoes, tomatoes or peppers. They came from other areas such as North America, so no one had heard of them!

Oh, and as a child on a farm, there was no school. You'd be out in the fields working hard as soon as you could walk.

TOP OF THE CROPS

1. BARLEY
   Good for making bread
2. RYE
3. OATS
4. BEANS ← *Good for making farts*
5. TURNIPS
   stinky

6. PEAS
7. CABBAGES YUK!
8. ONIONS
9. APPLES
10. BERRIES

As a Viking crop-farmer, you would be reliant on the weather to give your fields water and sun. Bad weather would mean failed crops (boo!), meaning you and your family could end up with a *berry* empty store cupboard over winter.

Animals were also crucial to

farmers, though most Vikings only ate the odd piece of meat (see page 24). Cows were number one as they provided milk (which could also be made into cheese, yum), followed by

I'm pretty big neeeeeeeews around here!

sheep, pigs and goats as well as chickens, ducks and geese (*egg*-cellent for eggs). Vikings near the coast or rivers also ate fish – they would pickle it or cover it in salt to keep it from going off.

It wasn't all hard work and grumbling tummies, though. Vikings who stayed at home had their community for support and occasional fun and games – perhaps even an invite to the local Jarl's hall for a special feast (see page 62). Hooray!

Raider

Haven't got any farmland? Struggling to feed yourself and your family? Why not join a band of fearsome Viking raiders?

As the number of Vikings grew, life got harder for many. Eldest sons would inherit their parents' farms, leaving younger siblings without many farming *crop*portunities. Heading out on a raid promised adventure (woo!), glory (yay!) and the chance of shiny treasure to bring home (ooh!).

Viking raiders may also have been recruited by kings or chieftains, who went looking for fearless men to accompany them overseas to look for

booty. (It was pretty much men only –
sorry, Gudrun, put that sword down.)

Packing light

You won't need to take much with you
on a raid (just as well, as you'd likely not
own much in the first place). Here are
some essentials . . .

I. Weapons

A sword is best – a spear or battle-axe
would do too. Some even brought bows
and arrows (great for long distance
fighting but not hand-to-hand combat).

You sure you can use that thing?

2. Warm clothes

A warm woollen cloak would have been a must for freezing nights at sea. Some Vikings wore clothing made of seal or other animal skins for extra warmth.

3. A sea chest

You might sit on this when rowing. On the outward journey it might contain food or clothes. On the return journey, it would (hopefully) be full of treasure!

4. Your sea legs

Viking longships were narrow and not very deep. This meant they could sail in shallow water, but in storms, they were tossed up and down by waves. Some seasick sailors became very vomity Vikings – yuck!

What's it to be? Are you a happy Viking home-bird? Or does sailing the seven seas sound much more fun? For more on Viking raids, head to page 12.

VIKING EXTRAS
Between worlds

The Vikings' view of Earth was very different to ours today. For starters, they thought the world was flat as a pancake and that four beardy dwarves called Norðri, Suðri, Austri and Vestri held up the sky. Let's take a tour . . .

Midgard

This was the home of humans. According to Viking myth, Midgard was surrounded by one big ocean, where a HUGE serpent called Jörmangandr lived. When we say huge, we're not kidding. He was long enough to completely surround Midgard!

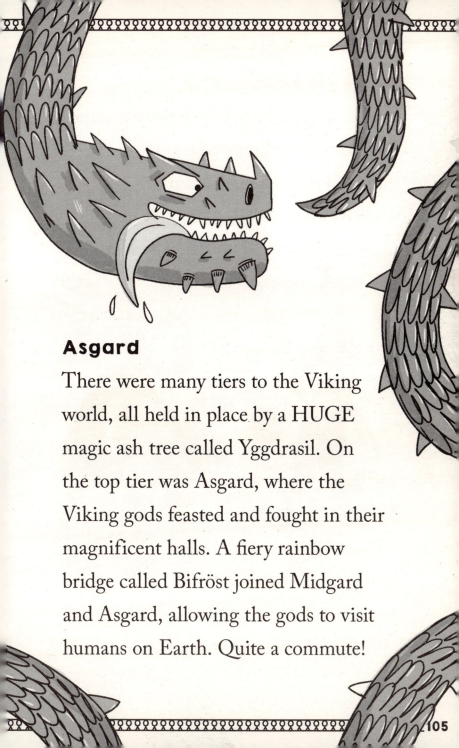

Asgard

There were many tiers to the Viking world, all held in place by a HUGE magic ash tree called Yggdrasil. On the top tier was Asgard, where the Viking gods feasted and fought in their magnificent halls. A fiery rainbow bridge called Bifröst joined Midgard and Asgard, allowing the gods to visit humans on Earth. Quite a commute!

Humans couldn't travel the other way as the bridge was guarded by the fearsome Heimdall, watchman of the gods. He had gold teeth, a giant horn to sound warnings, and hearing so good he could hear grass growing on the ground and wool growing on sheep. Baa!

Hel and Helvegr

Below Midgard lay Hel, a dark and mysterious underground world where

the dead lived. The goddess of Hel was
. . . Hel. This gloomy girl was not one
for parties – many sagas describe her
as cruel, severe and unsmiling. Not to
mention hideous – half of her body
was a skeleton, sometimes with a bit of
decaying flesh on it. Lovely.

Helvegr means the, "Road to Hel" –
anyone travelling along this highway,
would be dead. Unlucky. It's not all
doom and gloom though. Compared to
other religions and beliefs, the Vikings'
hell was a pretty normal place – the dead
farmed, explored and feasted, much as
they did in life.

Hel
(Turn off
next left)

WOULD YOU RATHER

meet the world's best warriors in Valhalla

OR meet Loki and his team of trickster gods in Ragnarök?

UNLIKE THE WORLD OF HUMAN VIKINGS, THE VIKING GODS LIVED IN A GLORIOUS WORLD OF MAGIC AND PLENTY – INCLUDING VALHALLA, A HUGE HALL BUILT BY ODIN AS A PLACE FOR GODS AND WARRIORS KILLED IN BATTLE. BUT DON'T GET TOO COMFORTABLE ... THE HUGE BATTLE OF RAGNARÖK IS ON ITS WAY!

Valhalla

Welcome to Valhalla! If you found yourself here, you'd likely be a brave and fearsome warrior killed in battle, or a god. Good for you, try out your best Viking warrior pose!

Valhalla was built by Odin, the king of the Viking gods (see page 126 for more on him). Legends describe it as an enormous hall with a roof made of razor-sharp Viking spears with golden shields for roof tiles. Fancy.

The Vikings believed that Valkyries (see page 128) transported

half of their fallen warriors to Valhalla, where they would live happily for the rest of their days. The other half were taken to Fólkvangr, a beautiful meadow ruled over by the goddess Freyja (see page 122).

Though, in theory, Valhalla was a place of rest for warriors, it wasn't all that restful. Unless fighting and feasting are your idea of relaxation, of course. Valhalla had a special practice yard

where the ghostly, fallen Vikings would
spend all day fighting each other for fun
(tough luck if you were a dead warrior
who thought their sword-swinging days
were behind them). Any wounds they
suffered would magically heal the same
day so they could fully enjoy an epic feast
throughout the night.

Food and drink never, ever ran out
during this feast. The Vikings' drinking
cups, made from animal horns, would
be constantly refilled with mead (a drink
made from honey). This came from the
udders of a magic goat called Heidrun,
who lived on the roof of Valhalla. Baaa.

Bonus fact:

Viking warriors in Valhalla would eat the meat of a boar that would magically come back to life the next day. That would be hard to *pig-nore*!

Ragnarök

Are you a prankster at heart? Would you rather be in one epic battle than constant fight-practice? Get ready for Ragnarök!

The Vikings believed that their gods (and humans with them) were destined for destruction in a huge, end-of-the-world battle called Ragnarök – meaning 'the doom of the gods'.

Ragnarök was a mysterious event. No one knew when it would begin, so you'd have to stay on your toes! A key sign was thought to be a series of years with cold, harsh winters in Midgard (the realm of humans).

This would be followed by the Sun and Moon being gobbled up by two hideous, giant wolves called Hati and Skoll.

It doesn't taste of cheese!

They believed the wolves' dramatic dining would cause the Earth to shake so much that any gods or people in prison would be broken right out. Among the jubilant prisoners would be the trickster god, Loki. (He'd annoyed the other gods so much they had chained him up in a cave. Sometimes, gods are no fun.)

The newly freed Loki's plan was to gather all the souls from Hel and sail with them towards Asgard, home of the gods (see page 105 for more). The ship the dead sailed in was called Naglfar and was made solely of fingernails and toenails of the dead. Yuck!

Loki's forces would then be joined by giants, yet another monstrous wolf called Fenrir (who was actually Loki's son) and the huge sea serpent, Jörmangandr that surrounded Midgard. It added up to quite some army of baddies!

Meanwhile, the gods in Asgard and all the fallen Vikings in Valhalla would be alerted that something fishy was going on by Heimdall, the watcher god, blowing his horn. They'd then know to prepare for the final battle. There would be some epic face-offs between Asgard's gods and their enemies:

RAGNARÖK
— BATTLE OF THE CHAMPIONS —

ODIN vs **FENRIR**
THE MONSTROUS WOLF

HEIMDALL vs **LOKI**

THOR vs **JÖRMANGANDR**
THE ENORMOUS SERPENT

FREYJA vs **SURTR**
THE FIRE GIANT

Spoiler alert: It was believed that nearly all of the giants, baddies and all of Asgard's big names including Thor and Odin would be killed in this battle.

What about the humans, you ask? Back in Midgard, the legend goes that only two humans survived – sorry. They managed it by climbing up a tree as the rest of the world sank into a boiling sea.

It all sounds pretty grim, eh? But there is hope. In the tale, a new world is created, new gods emerge and the offspring of the two people that shinned up the tree populate the Earth. Phew!

Are you ready to Ragna-rock and roll? Or maybe you'd rather go back to the land of human Vikings . . . go to page 94 if so!

Viking gods hall of fame

The Vikings had LOTS of different gods who all had different specialist roles, from holding up the sky to looking after fallen warriors to being in charge of love and marriage. They were the big shots of Viking religion before Christianity took over – so it's not surprising that their lives are central to the sagas (stories and historical accounts from Viking times). Read on to find out about a few of them!

Fabulous Freyja
Goddess of love and happiness

Being the goddess of such joyful things as love and happiness, Freyja must have had a pretty lovely life. Her family was equally delightful – she had a twin brother called Freyr who was the god of peace and fertility, helping farmers' crops to grow.

She was said to be incredibly beautiful and in some sagas, all the male gods fancied her! But she wasn't just a pretty face and had brains as well as beauty – she was a master of *seidr* magic, a mystical power that allowed her to look into the future. Watch out!

Freyja usually rode around in a chariot pulled by two cats. But, if she fancied a change, she'd ride on the back of her BATTLE BOAR, a giant golden bristled hog by the name of Hildisvini.

Freyja was also in charge of Fólkvangr – a land where half of the souls of Vikings killed in battle were sent (the other half travelled to Valhalla – see page 110). She also had a pretty epic wardrobe, including a special cloak of falcon feathers. Whoever got to wear it could fly!

With haste Mr Tibbles

Thunderous Thor
God of thunder

As the Norse god of thunder and lightning, it's maybe not very surprising that Thor was LOUD.

He was usually shown with a giant bushy beard and had a fierce temper, loving nothing more than a fight.

Thor was the strongest of all the Viking gods. Check out those bulging muscles – he didn't need to hit the gym. They came in very useful for handling his mighty hammer, called Mjölnir.

This could smash a mountain to smithereens with just a single strike! It wouldn't matter where or how far Thor flung Mjölnir, it would always come whizzing back into his hands like a very smart, heavy boomerang.

Thor was also the god of law and order – amazing when you think of all the mayhem he could cause. He would spend time sorting out matters of justice, racing across the sky in a chariot drawn by two gigantic goats. Baa. Viking people thought that it was this chariot that caused thunder!

Outrageous Odin
King of the Viking gods

Odin was one of the most important gods in Norse mythology – and he was a pretty distinctive guy. He had a long beard and cloak, and was usually accompanied by an assortment of animal friends – two ravens, Huginn and Mininn, and two wolves, Geri and Freki. They would act a bit like spies, bringing Odin useful titbits of information from the human world. He also only had one eye – he traded one for wisdom!

As well as being extremely wise (and having a very mysterious wizardy vibe), Odin was a master poet, having used his sneaky skills to steal a special

potion called the Mead of Poetry from
some selfish giants – this potion gave
the drinker brilliant poetic ability! To
escape from the giants, Odin turned
himself into an eagle – but while he was
making his escape by air, some of the
potion fell to Earth as eagle poo. The
people who found this poo became the
world's terrible poets!

Valiant Valkyries
Escorts to the afterlife

The Valkyries weren't in the main gang
of gods like Odin, Freyja and Thor
– but they were an impressive bunch.
They were servants of Odin, and would
journey to battlefields to find dead
warriors worthy of entering Valhalla, a
heavenly palace just for Norse warriors
(see page 110). They would carefully
escort these warriors back to the palace,
where they would bring them goblets of
mead (a sort of wine made of honey).
A nice change from the battlefield!

The Valkyries would also be able to
decide warriors' fate in battle – so it was
better to stay on their good side . . .

Of course, this is just a small number of the many, many gods, goddesses and magical beings from Viking legend – but which gets your vote?

WOULD YOU RATHER

be banished from your town for your crimes

OR be sentenced to a trial by combat?

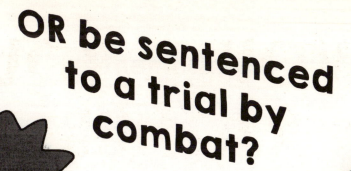

WITH ALL THE SLASHING AND SPEARING THEY DID ABROAD, IT'S NO WONDER THAT SOME VIKINGS ENDED UP ON THE WRONG SIDE OF THE LAW AT HOME. BUT VIKING COURTS WERE STRICT (SEE PAGE 72) — EVEN JUST SAYING THE WRONG THING COULD LAND YOU IN TROUBLE! AND THERE WERE SOME PUNISHMENTS YOU'D REALLY WANT TO AVOID . . .

Banishment

Think you could deal with a bit of solitude? Be careful, it might not be that peaceful out there . . .

Viking law worked a little differently to the systems of courts, judges, prisons and fines most countries use today. If the Thing (the Viking court – see page 74) decided a crime was serious enough, the perpetrater could end up being banished (made to leave their community) and becoming an outlaw. This might sound like a cool Viking cowboy, but it was serious stuff. They'd lose all their rights, so anyone could beat, steal from or even kill them, without a single bushy Viking eyebrow being raised. They'd have to look out for anyone they had annoyed! Many ended *leaf*-ing their life behind and hiding in the woods – they got the nickname *skógarmaðr*, "a man of the forest".

On the plus side, some outlaws did fairly well out of starting a new life. Head to page 42 to read about Erik the Red, a famous outlawed Viking who went adventuring!

Bonus fact:

At some points in time during the Viking era, writing a love poem to a woman was a crime, not a rhyme – it would result in you becoming an outlaw.

Trial by combat

Think you'd rule in a duel? Have you got mega sword skills? You might just succeed in a trial by combat!

If you insulted another Viking, you'd really better be prepared to back it up. A trial by combat, known as a Holmgang, could be called by the insulted person*.

*Unless they were a thrall – hurling insults at slaves was free!

BIG NOSE!

FISH BREATH!

COWARD!

The Holmgang was fought with swords on a small area of ground (around 2.5 square metres), marked out by cloaks or cow hides. It would be fought until one Viking gave up and left, until blood was drawn, or, in some cases, to the death. Yikes!

If either person failed to turn up, they were called a *níðingr* – the very WORST insult amongst the Vikings. It was like being called a coward, a cheat, a liar and a thief all at the same time. The cheek!

VIKING EXTRAS
Jobs board

Do you love spending time outdoors?
Have a knack for patching up cuts and
bruises? Whatever your particular skills,
there's a Viking job for you . . . read
on to discover a few options, whether
Viking-credible or Scandi-sgraceful!

BATTLE STATIONS!

Are you a *cut* above the rest? Do you know your way around a saw? Then perhaps you should consider a job as a battlefield surgeon. Chop, chop and apply now!

BURN, BABY, BURN!

Do you just want a quiet life away from the hustle and bustle of raiding and pillaging? Do you have a keen interest in burning stuff? Are you able to stay up for long hours with no sleep? Then you're just right for the job of a charcoal burner! Apply today and we'll give you all you need*.

*Must supply your own one-legged stool and living quarters.

WORK WANTED

I am Sven, a Viking with strong hands looking for work. I'm not fussed about getting my hands dirty and I'm not scared of getting hurt. Favourite pastimes include sipping nettle tea in my nettle pants.

FEELING SWAMPED?

Are you *bogged* down by life's reponsibilites? Do you wish to get really *stuck in* with a hands-on job? If you're iron-willed and eagle-eyed, then perhaps searching for bog iron in a swamp is your life's calling! Don't delay, come down to the swamp today!

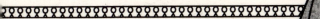

CHARCOAL BURNER

Place of work: The woods

Skills and qualities: Strong arms for lifting blocks of wood, patience, must enjoy spending time alone

Benefits: A (very) quiet life

Charcoal is wood that's been slowly burned so that all the water is removed from it. It was in BIG demand by Viking blacksmiths, as it was one of the few fuels that burned with enough heat for them to work iron and other metals to make their swords and tools.

As a charcoal burner, you'd live like a hermit in a shack or tent out in the woods. Hope you like camping! Here's how you'd make your charcoal:

STEP 1:

Gather a LOT of wood, stack it up, then cover it in ferns or moss. For every tonne of charcoal, you *wood* need a whopping four tonnes of wood.

STEP 2:

Heap earth over the big woody mound, then set light to it. Get comfortable – you'd need to watch it smoulder for four or five days.

STEP 3:

Pour water into the mound, watch it cool off and then dig out your charcoal! For your hard work, you'd get paid a tiny amount. You'd avoid being charged at on the battlefield though!

BATTLEFIELD SURGEON

Place of work: Viking battlefields

Skills and qualities: Physical strength, NOT squeamish, good at dodging arrows

Benefits: Meeting new people, helping other Vikings

Up for an exciting, action-packed life on the battlefield? Get your coat and let's get to work!

You'd need to make sure you don't mind anything too grisly. After a battle, the scene could be pretty *gore*-ful. If a Viking was lucky enough to escape with just a bad leg or arm wound, amputation may have been prescribed – enter the army's carpenter.

Wait, carpenter?! Hold on a second – weren't we talking about being a battlefield surgeon?

That's right. But Viking surgeons would need a carpenter's saw and other tools to perform operations. Eek!

As if that wasn't bad enough, there was no anaesthetic, and infections were common. Vikings tried to clean and dress wounds but their medical knowledge was limited, so only some people who had a leg removed survived.

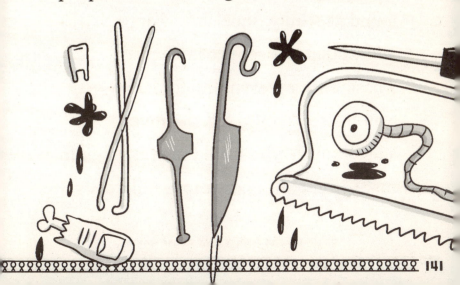

BOG IRON HUNTER

Place of work: Bogs, swamps and marshes

Skills and qualities: Not bothered by wet feet, enjoys being outdoors, eagle eyes

Benefits: Plenty of alone time, satisfaction of a good find

Maybe a bit of swampy scavenging would suit your skills? Hope you've got a good pair of wellies*!

Bog iron is a type of impure iron found in stinky, squelchy swamps and wetlands – some people made a basic living scavenging for it. Bog iron hunters would sell their wares to a blacksmith who would melt it down to make iron tools and weapons like axes.

*Oh wait – the Vikings didn't have wellies.

As a bog iron hunter you'd have to trudge off into the wetlands armed with little more than a stout stick and a sack. You'd poke your stick into the soft ground until you hit something hard. Then, you'd have to plunge your hands deep down into the squishy mud to pull the lump out.

Hope you like things damp – sometimes, you would wade through marshes and swamps up to your thighs in smelly sludge!

Are you ready to head outdoors and get scorching, sawing or searching? If you feel you've got an altogether more unusual set of skills, try page 144 . . .

WOULD YOU RATHER

be a battlefield berserker

OR a rune writer?

THE WORLD OF VIKING WORK WAS CERTAINLY BUSY – NO 9-5 DESK JOBS HERE! FROM FARM FIELDS TO SPEEDY SHIPS, THERE WAS ALWAYS PLENTY TO DO. SOME VIKINGS THOUGH, CHOSE SOME BIZARRE, MYSTERIOUS AND DOWNRIGHT DANGEROUS WAYS TO SPEND THEIR TIME . . .

Berserker

Do you fancy a wild life of travel and adventure? Are you a fearless risk-taker? Great! Let's get beserking . . .

Vikings didn't tend to go on more than one raiding and looting mission during their lives. Even though they were formidable fighters, there was a huge risk of ending up stone dead.

Despite this, a few (rash and foolhardy) Viking raiders worked themselves up into a wild frenzy as a raid or battle approached. They were called berserkers and were terrifying!

As their longships reached shore, some berserkers would howl and jump up and down, maybe even start ripping off their armour to fight naked. Historians think they may have eaten berries or plants that contained powerful drugs beforehand. They were often sent ahead of the main raid to swing their swords and create havoc.

Being a beserker was a risky business. With such little thought of their own safety, many berserkers didn't survive.

Rune writer

Do you prefer carving stones to breaking bones? Being a rune writer may be up your street!

Runes (meaning 'secret' or 'mystery') were a set of symbols representing sounds that made up the Vikings' alphabet. Not all of their letters were the same as our modern Roman alphabet – they didn't have a J, K or Q, for example, and had a couple of extras, such as single symbols for sounds like "th". To make things even more confusing, there were slightly different sets of runes used in different times and parts of the Viking world.

Here's one set of alphabet runes:

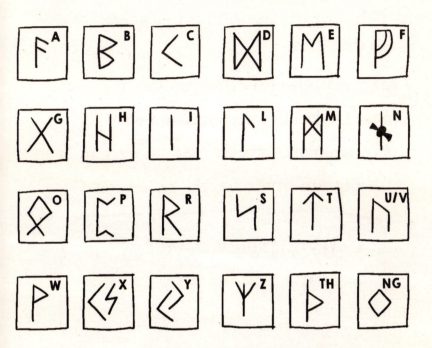

Runes weren't written on paper but instead carved into stone, wood or iron using a sharp chisel or knife. Mind your fingers! These hard materials made it difficult to shape round edges – that's why most runes only use straight lines.

Some large Viking stones were carved with tales of strong Viking leaders.

Why not try a bit of rune reading yourself? Use the runes on the previous page to decode the punchlines to these Viking jokes – check your answers at the bottom of the page!

1. Why didn't the Viking god go fighting the next day after a big battle?

His body was too ᚦᛟᚱ

2. Why was the Viking longship so cheap?

It was on ᛋᚨᛁᛚ

3. Who was head librarian at the Viking library?

Eric the ᚱᛗᚠᛇ

4. Why didn't the Viking go raiding?

Because he didn't want to ᛚᛖᛁᚹ *home*

5. Where are Viking babies put once they're born?

In a ᚾᛟᚱᛋᛖ*-ry*

6. What do you call a lavish Viking?

A big ᛋᚢᛖᚾ *-der*

So, what's it to be? Are you ready to carve something *runebelievable,* or go beserk? If you'd rather be on the farm than risking harm, go to page 96 . . .

How it all ended

Like many other civilisations, it's hard
to put a finger on an exact date when
the Viking age ended – it was more
of a slow fizzling out than a big
explosive 'BANG' of an ending.

There was one important final battle
though – the Battle of Stamford Bridge
in Yorkshire, England, in 1066. Viking
king Harald Hardrada got his best
gang of Vikings together and tried
to invade England. He was VERY
confident – Harald and his men didn't
expect to meet much resistance, so
didn't even bring much armour with
them to the battle. Unsurprisingly, they

were no match for Saxon king, Harold Godwinson, who had a large, sensibly well-armoured squad of soldiers.

Of course, the Vikings didn't vanish off the face of the Earth, axes, beards and all, after this battle. They just gradually stopped raiding. England and other European countries had developed large, hairy and scary armies, making them frankly annoying to attack. Many Vikings gave raiding a hard pass, and stayed at home instead.

The Viking legacy lives on, though. Some English words, like 'freckle', 'egg' and 'cake' come from the Norse language. Remember that next time you're tucking into a Battenburg!

Glossary

Anglo-Saxons – an ancient people who lived in modern-day England in the early middle ages.

Asgard – a level of the Viking universe home to the Viking gods.

Berserker – a Viking warrior sent ahead of an army to terrify the opposition.

Boss – the central part of a shield.

Blacksmith – a person whose job is to work metal to make tools or weapons.

Chain mail – a type of armour made of lots of interlinked metal rings.

Fólkvangr – a field ruled by the goddess Freyja, where half of dead warriors went (the other half went to Valhalla).

Hel – the Viking underworld.

Holmgang – a trial by combat.

Hnútukast – a Viking game involving throwing bones.

Jarl – a Viking chief or leader.

Longhouse – a Viking home.

Longship – a type of Viking ship propelled by oars and sails.

Longsword – a type of sword with a double edged blade.

Midgard – a level of the Viking universe home to humans.

Norse – a language spoken by Vikings.

Runes – Symbols used in Viking writing.

Ragnarök – an event in Viking mythology that would mark the end of the world.

Saga – Viking legends, stories and historical accounts from the time.

Scandinavia – an area of northern Europe where the Vikings came from, including modern-day Norway, Denmark, Sweden and Iceland.

Skald – a Viking poet.

Thrall – a Viking slave.

Toga Honk – a Viking tug-of-war game.

Valhalla – a grand hall ruled by the god Odin, where half of dead warriors were transported by Valkyries (the other half went to Fólkvangr).

Valkyrie – a magical winged woman who guided fallen warriors to Valhalla.

Yggdrasil – a huge tree thought to be in the centre of all levels of the Viking universe.

About the author

Clive Gifford is not quite as old as the Vikings and certainly nowhere near as fierce. He has been intrigued by their history and deeds ever since visiting the Jorvik Viking Centre in York which recreates the sights, sounds (and the smells!) of the Norse, of course. Clive has written more than 200 books for children and adults, and has won the Royal Society, SLA and Blue Peter book awards. He lives in Manchester, UK.

About the illustrator

As a young boy, Tim Wesson was constantly doodling, finding any excuse to put pen to paper. Since turning his much loved pastime into his profession, Tim has achieved great success in the world of children's publishing, having illustrated and authored books across a variety of formats. He takes great delight in turning the world on its head and inviting children to go on the adventure with him.

Explore the rest of the series for more fascinating facts and hilarious would you rather questions!